To: Michelle

From: Your Verizon Pals
June 2015

NAUGHTY
BETTY
PRESENTS

IT'S ALL
GOING
TO BE
OKAY-ISH

A LITTLE BOOK OF HUMOR THERAPY

SELLERS
PUBLISHING

DEDICATION
To all the ladies in the trenches

Published by Sellers Publishing, Inc.

Copyright © 2015 Naughty Betty, Inc.
All rights reserved.

Sellers Publishing, Inc.
161 John Roberts Road, South Portland, Maine 04106
www.sellerspublishing.com • E-mail: rsp@rsvp.com
ISBN 13: 978-1-4162-4551-3

10 9 8 7 6 5 4 3 2 1
Printed and bound in China.

TRUST US.
The crazy deadlines, the visible roots,
the lack of "likes" on your Facebook page—
all that stuff is just life happening.
And that's a good thing. It means you are alive
and well and living in the real world. So on
those days—when you forget to shave the other
leg, or the dog eats a couch cushion,
or you see a friend having an epic fail—grab
this little book. Share a laugh. Maybe even
a snort. And remember that you're blissfully
happy once in a while. That you're human.
That in five years—maybe even five days—
this drama will seem hilarious.
IT'S ALL GOING TO BE OKAY-ISH.

YOU COULD BE A
TODDLER
IN A
TIARA

CELEBRATE
WHETHER
YOUR

CALENDAR LIKES IT OR NOT

TEN
POUNDS
YOUNGER

ACT LIKE A
LADY
BITCH

OH FOR GOD'S SAKE

EAT SOME GLUTEN

AVOID BEING OVER SCHEDULED

AND
UNDER
CHARDONNAYED

ANYTHING IS POSSIBLE WITH

WINE AND A GOOD CONCEALER

YOU'D
MAKE A
TERRIBLE
NUN

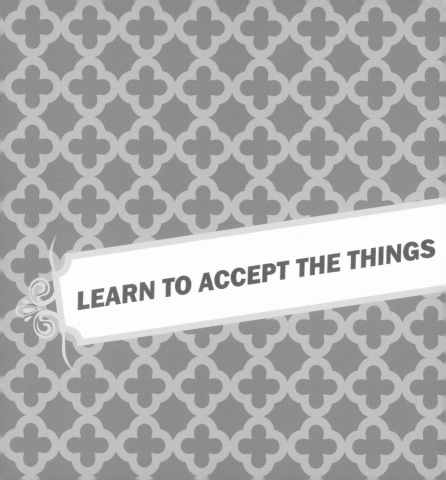

LEARN TO ACCEPT THE THINGS

THE SALON CAN'T CHANGE

THEN LET'S CALL
CELLULITE
THE NEW
TATTOO

BY THE
WORD
MA'AM

REMEMBER THAT
WITH
MONEY
AND
MEDICATION

YOU'D
BE
UNSTOPPABLE

SCREW THE MIDLIFE CRISIS.

GO HAVE A MIDLIFE TIRAMISU.

MEN FANTASIZE ABOUT YOU, AND CHILDREN OBEY YOU

YOU CAN
SURVIVE
ANYTHING

AS OFTEN AS
YOUR
HORMONES

THERE'S A
PILL
FOR
EVERYTHING

WHO CARES WHAT
YOUR
BOOBS
LOOK LIKE

TO CHEAT AT
YOGA

BOLDLY
REJECT THE
WORLD

OF THE
SKIRTED
BATHING
SUIT

WHEN
CARBS
AND
TELEVISION
WEREN'T *SO* EVIL

WHEN
BAD
THINGS
HAPPEN

CALL
GOD
AND SAY
DUDE
WTF

KNOW THAT
WE ALL
HAVE
DAYS

WHEN WE'RE
ONE
GOODIE
BAG
SHORT

AS A
CELEBRITY
WITH HER
ORIGINAL
NOSE

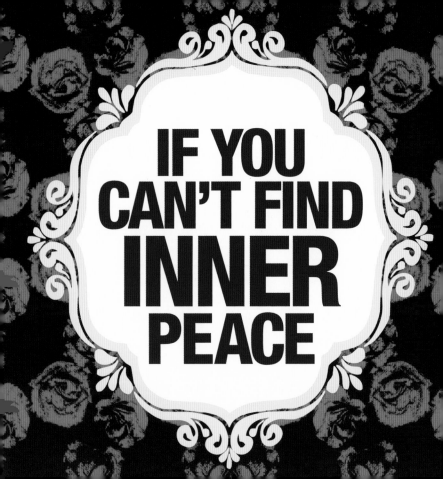

LOOK FOR A
CLEARANCE
RACK

BE A SEQUIN IN A

WORLD OF KHAKI

WOW, MONEY REALLY CHANGED HER

GIVE YOURSELF A NEW
SHOE-
GASM

LIKE ALL THOSE *BILLIONAIRE* *SELF-HELP* *GURUS*

FOLLOWED BY A
MUSCLE
RELAXER